MEMORY AND RAIN

MEMORY AND RAIN

poems

JIM NATAL

 RED HEN PRESS | Los Angeles, California

ISBN: 978-1-59709-136-7

Library of Congress Catalog Card Number: 2008940755

Design and layout by Amanda Sowards

Front cover painting: John Register (1939-1996), "Pacific Coast Highway," 1990. Courtesy Modernism Gallery, San Francisco

www.modernisminc.com

The California Arts Council, the Los Angeles County Arts Commission, the National Endowment for the Arts, and the City of Los Angeles Department of Cultural Affairs partially support Red Hen Press.

First Edition

Published by Red Hen Press

www.redhen.org

ACKNOWLEDGMENTS

Grateful thanks to the editors of the following journals and anthologies for publishing these poems, sometimes in slightly different forms:

Art/Life: "The Red Door"; *Askew*: "Blur"; *Bellingham Review*: "Photographic Memory"; *Cider Press Review*: "Layover"; *Eclipse*: "Dan Marino's Quick Release"; *Pool*: "Animal Planet"; *Reed*: "52"; *Runes*: "Rain in L.A.—Thursday Morning," "Three Fates," and "Travelers"; *SOLO Café*: "Still Life from Memory"; *The Los Angeles Review*: "Rain in L.A.—Sunday"; *Windfall*: "On Broken Top: Three Sisters Wilderness"; "Borderline" appears in the anthology *Mischief, Caprice, and Other Poetic Devices* (Red Hen Press, 2004); "Filter" appears in *Blue Arc West, An Anthology of California Poets* (Tebot Bach Press, 2006); "Lost: One Footed Adult Crow. Reward" was a winner in the 2003 Poetry in the Windows Prize Competition sponsored by the Arroyo Arts Collective; "The Missing Scene: He Speaks Again to the Ghost of His Father" appears in the anthology *Chance of a Ghost* (Helicon Nine Editions, 2005); Section IV of "In Memory of Her Memory" appears in *Beyond Forgetting: Poetry and Prose About Alzheimer's Disease* (Kent State University Press); "Unleavened" was one of the winners of the 2005 Poetry Postcards Competition sponsored by Writers at Work and supported by a grant from the L.A. Arts Commission.

Special thanks to David St. John, and to my teachers, mentors, and friends Chris Abani, Frank Gaspar, Eloise Klein Healy, Steve Heller, Carol Potter, and Susan Terris, all of whom offered inspiration and insight for the poems in this collection.

For all those who have lifted me in their Atlas arms.
And, especially, for Tania.

CONTENTS

Rain in L.A.

Art will never be able to do without nature.
When one forgets everything,
all that remains is oneself and that is not enough.
—Pierre Bonnard

Rain in L.A.

Thursday morning

This is a dialogue town,
hard-boiled repartee in a soft-boiled climate.
The mountains wisecrack to the desert,
while the Santa Anas, the red winds,
wring their raspy hands, snivel and sweat
like Peter Lorre waiting for a call on a
black phone from the fat, accented ocean,
the brains behind the operation.
Here, nobody goes out when it rains.
Authors read to the backs of empty chairs.
The movies talk to themselves.
Does the whole city steal
that rare chance to stay home, to listen
to weather spackling the windows,
"So What" softly in the background,
drink and shrink the stack of magazines
beetled beside the bed? Are they all
afraid of hydroplaning on the 405,
upturned SUVs and jack-knifed trailers,
highway patrol cops in yellow slickers
erecting shrines of flares?
Or do people think they'll melt
like the wicked witch of the coastal west,
leave nothing but a grounded broom
and a puddle on an empty soundstage as if
it's 1939 in Culver City? Oh, man,
it's raining munchkins and there are evil
clouds of flying monkeys rumbling in.

Thursday evening

Cracks in the pavement fill to overflowing,
bring up the worms of remorse,
the insidious Southern California pink ones that,
hours later under the unavoidable sun,
turn gray to the consistency of ruptured
rubber bands around old bank statements. Too nice.
People tell me that. Friends. My wife.
I hate it—wish it were different, that my father
wasn't the nice guy everyone liked. How much
did he *need* to be liked? Do I? I always wanted
to intimidate: a pair of mirrored sunglasses
strangers think twice about approaching.
Clipped. Prickly. Lank. Taut. Buzz-cut silver.
Got your mind right, Luke?

But my soft wiring is more treacherous than Iago.
Especially when it rains for days in black-and-white
and regrets crawl out like mutant ants
from storm drains, flood cement banks
of once-upon-a-time rivers that still can flash
from runoff to rage in minutes and flush the stashed
bodies from all over the city into the harbors,
"floaters" the police say are hell to identify
because they could have died anywhere,
could have been anyone.

Middle of the night

Inadequacies spew from every pore
as if I'm sweltering in a cheap suit and tie
in the orchid hothouse of old money.
Sleep is out of the question, the foghorn
as incessant as the stuttering of the rain.
Between storm cells in the afternoon I walked
the footpath along the speckled canal, a miniature
man dodging raindrops. The egrets
wore their stilts and stabbing masks.
A blue heron, taller than I, took flight—
so effortless, such slow and graceful wings.
And suddenly I was underwater in Belize following
that slate gray spotted ray, soaring above
brain coral, not caring if my breath held out, the ray
so slow and graceful and absolutely siren beautiful,
drawn beyond the dropoff to the Caribbean deep.
I'm in over my head, that's for sure.
The cat beside me stirs. She spends more time
asleep than awake, life lived inside out.
But isn't that how I live?
Asleep through the waking parts, awake
here in bed, listening to the rain, the rain,
the shit coming down so hard you have to wear a hat.

Friday dawn

The crows are up early, already yakking to themselves and anything
within earshot, winged lunatics in black trenchcoats twisting
twigs off the wet, not-yet-budding branches with ebony nutcracker beaks.
Even they, annoying, troubling in their recent profusion, make nests.
I should know better than to listen to blues on a stormy morning
grayer than a South Chicago back porch. I should know a lot of things.
The eagle flies on Friday, the song goes, except here, still out of work
and scrambling, burning both ends to make the middle meet while
countless billions pelt foreign cities with shrapnel and hot lead.
Oh yeah, *blues is my business and business is good.*

In my version of L.A., everything is as the crow flies, seeking
a dead reckoning. *I'm so broke right now I can't even spend the night.*
The red kettle on the stove spits and sizzles. The grinder whines.
I ordered coffee but the blues poured me misery. I pour extra
grounds into the paper cone. Forget caffeine.
Staying up is not the problem. Nor is hearing the hiss
of the building sprinklers come on at 4 A.M.,
timer oblivious to hours of soaking, the sated
lawn regurgitating while *I feel like I'm drowning on dry land.*
Drivers' doors open, latch closed, the ignitions of first risers
leaving for jobs in near dark. Even then the freeways won't be free.
All this anger welling: *Somebody got to suffer,*
somebody sure got to feel some pain. I wish I could wring
screeching blues out of the neck of some scarred guitar, amps sparking,
short-circuiting in this everlasting downpour, pissed-
off neighbors raising windows, shouting, "You better be careful
out in that rain or...*you may wash your life away.*"

Friday late afternoon

"A close call for Earth this week."
That's what the newscaster said.
An asteroid, lone wolf of the solar system,
passed between the Earth and moon within
26,000 miles, a few concentric rings away
from a spot-on blue bullseye. I know how
that 100-foot chunk of space spindrift feels:
not a failure exactly, but not a complete
success. The TV showed artist's renderings
of huge explosions, dying dinosaurs, and aerial
photographs of the impact crater near Winslow,
Arizona, where that flatbed Ford, my Lord,
slowed down so many years, whoa, make that
decades ago. There were movie clips, too—
a pathetic but valiant last-ditch human
attempt to save the planet with a pre-emptive
nuclear strike against an alien drive-by,
the dark-tinted windows already rolled down.
You know, blow it up before
it blows us up, blah, blah, blah....
as if there's a way to dodge when God's
throwing rocks. Right now, though,
wicked rain is the imminent threat, driving
down with such force it's raining up,
like I'm standing on a platform between
two trains running and neither is going my way.
On the screen are Valley yea-sayers
with plastered hair and squishing shoes,
their cars stalled engine-block-deep in intersections,
sputtering "We need it. We *need* it"
while getting drenched for the third

of potentially 40 days and nights in a row.
We need it, all right.
And I'm not talking about rain.

Saturday morning

The rain trails a sodden bridal train whipped
by ocean blasts—blown south from the wet
Cascades, east from Japan and the Pacific islands,
up from the Gulf of California
with mango-scented moisture.

In the wake of the wind, there's an obstacle course
of downed dead and brown fronds, fallen from the heights
of pencil-necked palms. You never hear of joggers killed
by sawfish-billed planks dropping,
a curse of rattling wooden brooms, prosthetic
arms and hands pointing up Ocean Avenue toward
mudslide-prone paths atop the Santa Monica bluffs.
Maybe dented car roofs and hoods
are too common to mention. And not even
the most endorphin-obsessed runner is out there now.

Still, you can only stay socked-in so long in
a shuttered hotel before something swells to bursting.
From a drawer, a gun, a newly refilled prescription,
last week's TV listings. Re-runs again.

Everyone thinks of palm trees when that "I Love L.A."
song comes on—convertible Benz's and Bentleys swinging
into crushed white shell driveways of stucco pink hotels,
valet jockeys in vests lining the curbs
like perfect pickets of *Washingtonia Robusta*, saturated
watercolor brushes swathing a sunset sky
or boulevard.

Rats thrive among the withered palm fringe, as do squirrels,
and occasional flocks of crème de menthe parrots
that play one night stands in these urban tropics,

doing their stubby Groucho walk
head-down on the trunks, outsquawking the leafblowers
gusting for minimum wage when
the wind does the job
for free.

Saturday sunset

Lorca writes: "They do not think
of the rain and they've fallen asleep
suddenly as if they were trees." I don't
think of the rain either. It *isn't* raining.
Somerset Maugham never wrote "Rain."
I think I'll go to the carwash.
There is no such thing as rain or evolution.
No drizzle, spatter, drip, or seep.
No water stains. No swishing branches,
brushes on cymbals riffing
in river-cryin' jazz lounge time.
We don't need no stinking umbrellas,
no newspapers folded into sinking
upturned boats, inky runnels of hard
luck stories streaming down faces
and the backs of necks. I refuse
to believe in the afterlife of rain,
in drowned angels or Lucifers, no bibles
crumbling like soggy matchbooks.
There is no poetry in the rain,
no reason to bother thinking up
even 17 syllables about it. I hear
no music in the rain on a tin roof,
no rodent scuttling, fingertapping,
teeth clacking, hammer pounding,
machine gunning steel band calypso
against the windows. I do the limbo
under the rain. I fly below the radar
of the rain. I laugh in the face of you, Rain.
I'm wearing rain-patterned camouflage;

the rain falls right by me, can't see me.
And what if it could?
I've become the rain, made a friend
of rain, am one with the rain. It rains,
therefore I am.

Saturday night

I'm sick to death of rain. I'm so very tired of it. Who'll stop this rain
if I don't? And I'm just too exhausted. No, I mean *weary*. I'm as weary
as "The Swede" lying fully dressed in weary clothes on a weary ticking
mattress lumped on weary creaking springs, smoking weary cigarettes
in stale and weary darkness waiting wearily for heavy footsteps
on weary stairs, hard upon the worn, weary carpeting of the long
and weary hall, unlocked door to the weary flophouse room flung open;
lightning chased by two shots of thunder.

Sunday

At six in the morning
  exactly six in the morning.
The rain is gone
  leaving an exit wound.
The rain is gone
  like an assassin.
The rain is gone
  shouldn't there be church bells?
The rain is gone
  taking half the bed with it.
The rain is gone
  my first friend went down when I was 15 years old.
The rain is gone
  serves me right to suffer, serves me right to be alone.
The rain is gone
  you awaken written in blue tattoos.
The rain is gone
  a case of mistaken identity.
The rain is gone
  a case of amnesia.
The rain is gone
  like the last plane to Lisbon.
The rain is gone
  they're dragging the rivers.
The rain is gone
  on the lam in Mexico.
The rain is gone
  the fix was in.
At six in the morning
  exactly six in the morning.
The rain is gone
  until the next time.

The rain is gone
　　won't *be* a next time.
The rain is gone at six in the morning:
　　Forget it, Jake, it's Chinatown.

Noon

The fronts have moved on, dealing
early monsoons to northern Arizona, dampening
the streets of Phoenix, discomfort index
raised to double digits. It's their turn now,
and perhaps they've got it coming.
Well, we've all got it coming, don't we, an endless
batting order until we're called out on strikes
or fear strikes out or we walk,
whichever comes first.

Put the blame on the rain, boys. You can't blame
the dead. Every day is *Dia de los Muertos* around here
and all the sugar skulls dissolved.
Gale-force ghosts have scattered
the rosary petals, snuffed out the votives.
The dead are no help anyway. They don't talk back
and the empty car seat beside me stays empty,
missing a golden opportunity for a chat.

And, speaking of golden, I see the lighting crew
is back at work. That diffused citrus aura
that is too, too L.A. surrounds the city
with *faux* afterglow. Of course, it's an illusion—
the same *deus-ex-smog* that animates our sunsets—
and it's as temporary as distant snowcaps viewed
from the intersection of Pico and Sepulveda.
Pi-co and Se-pul-veda. Pi-co and Se-pul-veda.

What isn't an illusion? Palm trees are an illusion,
piercing the haze and sprawl,
the quintessential establishing shot.
Palm trees behind the opening titles: must be

Beverly Hills, Venice Beach, Santa Monica.
Look! It's the Hollywood sign. But here's the scoop:
palms are trees the way toy poodles are dogs:
they throw no shade; they make lousy firewood;
they don't even have branches to hang yourself from.

Today, however, prisoners will be allowed to keep
their belts because this day wants to live.
Windchimes ping in harmony. Fluorescent
bougainvillea billow in jasmine-scented breezes
and impatiens shake themselves like spaniels.
Banana plants unfurl new fans, green
cormorant wings upraised and drying.
And there's a new bird-of paradise bloom, a white one,
hiding among the stalks and steaming stems.

By the ocean, the sand is Sahara-rippled, like perfect abs
or, for those inclined to a darker view, the beach
has been scoured until ribs show through. The Pacific
chatters in short sets and flat-hulled clouds
scud inland, passing gulls and boats in the channel
cruising the other way. Rigging clangs against masts.
And it's so clear you can stroll the jetty and count
millionaire houses on the Palisades.

In other words, it's a gorgeous day. Yet,
the memory of rain hounds me with a phantom itch.
You can't trust clouds in this city—
they dissipate in the sun, then re-form and barge in,
open up like tommy guns for days on end.
And there I am again, the pool man's nightmare,
floating behind the moldering mansion,

suspended face-down among storm litter and leaves,
a speck in backyard turquoise as seen from space.
But there's a certain L.A. *cachet* to that,
a *denouement* with…
grace.

Picking Fruit in the Dark

Away—away
into this hundred year life and beyond,
my story and I vanish together like this.
            —T'ao Ch'ien

Memory and Rain

Time's whispers are suspect, memory forever as much poet as reporter.
—James Sallis

Almost made it,
asleep through the night.
Nudged awake by the sound of rare rain at 4.
I wonder where the swallowtail we saw will weather,
yellow scalloped wings folded, trembling, drawn back
amid the lilac-shaped, lilac-colored spindles
of the butterfly bush. A moth
flies through the outdoor light instead,
thick-bodied, inelegant.

I have no choice
what passes into that light—
javelinas, deer, coyotes trotting their rounds,
jackrabbits the size of beagles.
Sent so that I'll see them or is it
intersection, pure lottery ball coincidence?
Is there purpose to this parade?
They walk through whether I'm up or not.

I remember lilacs.
Indiana summers, branches heavy as breasts
with purple fragrance, our ladies of the dunes.
My father's heart eruption.
My sister's baseball teeth, 50 years later deadening.
My dog, dead on the beach road, then lifted
in my father's arms. The night of the mountain lion
(my adopted spirit animal), escaped
from some peeling-paint traveling zoo,
a single cry reverberating and saucer prints
in the sand, the fat local cops having second thoughts
about tracking it in the morning.

The rain
has become a wet echo.
Our trees are happy this monsoon summer.
I'm happy (at least I think I am, despite…) No,
I should try to get back to sleep, an exponential list
tomorrow. I mean today, drafting so close
behind yesterday that if it stopped suddenly
there'd be a 50-car pile-up on the interstate.
A new watch for my birthday parses
time passing, time remaining. Only a dream,
and the memory of a dream at that.

But I follow:
from the beach on Lake Michigan
to Santa Fe to the beach at Marina del Rey.
Now Arizona (all beach and no ocean).
My daughter almost 21. Me almost 60,
the distant mesas in dawn relief. I'm living
the westerns I used to watch in black & white
(Range Rider, Johnny Mack, Roy and Gene,
Gabby chewing his shredded wheat beard, the skimpy-
masked Lone Ranger with his opera overture theme) .

Walking backward through the brush I cut a switch,
erase my tracks behind me as I go, knowing
there's always a Tonto who can read the trail.
In the middle of some nights it's me.

The First Story I Ever Wrote

was about a cowboy
sitting on his horse
on top of a hill
above a town
thinking about whether
he should ride down
(*here he unbuttons*
his cowboy shirt pocket
takes outs a paper
he's been keeping there)
because he's sure that
going into the town
is the last thing
that he'll ever do
and I don't recall
why death is so certain or
if a girl's waiting
and whether the cowboy
lets go of his reins
or spurs on his pinto
(*who at that point in life*
is his only true friend)
or if he does anything
except refold the poster
(*Wanted Dead or Alive*
with his picture on it)
or tilt down his hat brim
or feel for his rifle
strong in its scabbard and
I try to remember
if his saddle was creaking
or the horse's bit jingled

or the smell of the rain
mingled with sagebrush
or if he decides
to ride on or away
but 40 years later
shifting my weight
in this big leather chair
I'm back on a hill
and the killers are waiting
and I should have
lived long enough
to know.

You Awaken

1.

You awaken
written in blue tattoos,
every lifetime pain endured,
indigo joy
of living on this earth,
etched in lines that stretch
and fade with breath,
elastic and resilient,
scars set in ink,
tiny bloodpricks,
that heal over, form
the narrative arc of your body,
monochrome blue chapters
that won't wash off
in the rain. Oh,
they're yours—you
can see them in the mirror
where reversal of *truth*
almost spells *hurt*,
there upon your left chest
just below your shoulder.

2.

You awaken
written in blue tattoos,
dreams pried wide open.
The museum
has been looted, relics now
simply old bones, the dig
just holes in the sand;
instead of finds,
mounds of shards in the heat,
not worth enough shattered
to piece together.
This is what it's come to.
This is where
you try to wake up, skin
etched like a Durer plate,
a resolute knight
staring down the morning.
Death hunches beside the road
and the Devil beckons
with crooked blue fingers,
needles for nails,
impervious to sunlight.

3.

You awaken
written in blue tattoos.
This was not the vision
you prepared your spirit for—
past in front, future behind,
always quicker than you
no matter how fast you spin...
And you're slowing down,
law of entropy unbroken.
Around your forearms
tree limbs twine
in place of veins,
blue branchings of the elm
outside your childhood
bedroom window.
(Remember the faces
hidden in its leaves?)
Your biceps are bound
with short blue feathers,
(fledglings you found
and nursed to death).
On your palms are eyes
(close them and you make a fist).
And on both thighs incised
designs from Hebrew texts:
Lion of Judah; Ark of the Covenant;
pillar of fire; cave of Moses
covered by the hand of God;
the desecration
and the temple that must be rebuilt
each and every morning.

The Missing Scene: He Speaks Again to the Ghost of His Father

Do not turn your back on me and point to all the junctions
I have missed through sheer spirit lethargy, ebb of vision,
and lack of your favorites, *drive* and *determination*.

Do not remind me on this platform, cold and sick at heart,
of my fallings, too quick to quit, to cut my meager losses,
my denial of your faith, my failure to construct a temple,
as your father did before you, or to become, like you,
a pillar that even Samson could not pull down.

I am shackled to pillars of my own. But you should know that,
you, with your rear-view vision through the ether.

Clear, clear.

Eleven years not a sign from you, not a simple manifestation
no matter how low I scraped, how much I needed righteous
counsel. And now that my mother has passed over,
you return again just this once, you say. But I know different.
You ride me like a mule, burdened with your example.

Oh, how I wish I could follow you at first scent of morning,
first weaseling of the light. But that would be giving in again.

Not yet, not yet.

Were you this tired, this disgusted, as purpled bags began
to accumulate beneath the eyes, as biceps and thighs shrink back

from athletic grace, hair white and thinning, falling everywhere,
mortal scalp exposed and true shape of the skull revealed?

Did you consciously choose not to examine too closely, keep
your eye on the living and not on the life—children, house, job,
marriage a mantra loud enough to drown every mermaid,
art a distraction condoned, though forbidden by the prayer book;
separate dishes for milk and meat, business and poetry.

Compared to you—always compared to you—I am directionless.
There is no magnetic north anymore, my soul a lode of ferrous ore
that sets the needle spinning. Is there is no rest from it?
I was slow that morning, complacent and late to your bedside.

Forgive, forgive.

Lost: One-Footed Adult Crow. Reward.

Maybe it should have said "FREE" instead of "LOST."
Maybe it's the same crow I hear down the block
puncturing the morning with insistent counterpoint
to the soap-smooth Sunday dove songs.
And "LOST" to whom? One creature's lost
is another's escape. But now that it's back
among the power lines and madronas, this crow
really could be adrift, homeless and dressed
in shabby black, roosting in doorways
wrapped in atrophied wings.

There's the obvious question of how the crow lost
its foot, what led to its pet name of Hopalong, Gimpy,
or, perhaps, Lefty. Did it happen when it was young or grown?
Or was it born that way, its whole life a balancing act?
Crows are so smart. Curiosity or boredom
could have gotten the better of it. And with sharp-edged
suddenness, the idea of spending its maturity in someone's care
became more necessary than ludicrous: kind words,
a guaranteed ear, the certainty of scheduled meals,
a place to sleep with both eyes closed.

And about that reward: If the crow is returned,
accepts again its cage and perch or even comes back
on its own to reclaim its low-ceilinged kingdom,
will it be win-win all around? The owner regains
a live-in jester. The crow can relax, take a load off its foot.
And the alert-hearted Samaritan, who at first
refused the crisp twenty, now slips it in
with the other bills on the way down the back stairs.
It's almost like one of those Asian teaching tales—
how the unfortunate open window leads in as well as out.

VASE WITH RAMPANT LIONS

The blue of China wends silk roads to Syria and Samarra,
enters the bloodstreams of artisans. Patterns of lotus petals,

blue streamside pavilions, and billowing dragons are rendered
into palm trees and camels, paired birds and Koranic cursive.

Technique and hue drift like artful sediment,
layer upon layer settling north and east, where

Italian guildsmen equate cowry shell to the curve of
a young sow's back, and *porcelain* survives the journey

intact, still translucent, is assimilated and awaits
the arrival of Egyptian glass on Murano's shore.

Hummingbirds don't know what day it is
or the name of their nectar source.

Stork flocks wing to the rooftops of Delft.
Blue windmills churn in the charged air.

Sunset, Lake Como

For Montale

And now the church bells of Lenno
play their clumsy, one-note arpeggios.
Lake ducks *quack-a quack-a* to themselves
knowing anything is possible
once operatic orange clouds exit
the peaks for the night.

My thoughts struggle to join the moonrise,
just the other side of full. Twilight
deepens to *nero* and red wine is sipped
with *bresciola* and *formaggi stagioni*.
Dear Eugenio, this is your country
but this is not your place.

And now doubt descends, heavy and musty
as alter curtains. It was embedded here before you
were born, strata pressed into place, treacherous
lake road crimped between rock faces
and villa walls. Tourist busses and trucks can't
pass each other in places and the *carabinieri*
must halt traffic to allow them to back up
and wheel around for the return to Como.

Such daily beauty for these families, fortunes
framed by columns and brocade; the view north
toward Belaggio and Varenna, the high
vines of the Valtellina, their metaphor and currency.
Of course, the most magnificent villas are
in public trust now, the gardens suitably ambled,
picnics of foreign appreciation and the jealousy
of centuries that can't be turned.

＊

But it *is* changing, isn't it Eugenio? You can see
it in the cities especially, your famous ditches
writhing with new eels. And along the autostrada
on the way to Mont Blanc, at the gas stop
tagged large with "No Islam!" graffiti,
where the handsome Egyptian man
asks directions to Geneva.

＊

You played with time, braiding it like bride's hair,
plaiting past and present, all of it borrowed
and, ultimately, dark blue as the depths of cosmos
silhouetting the rim of stone that detains
this wishbone lake. Does the sky mirror the water
or the water the sky; smeared lights of stars and
Milan-bound jets, lanterns at the ends of floating docks
on the lone isle of Comancina, and zig-zagging
pin-dot ports and starboards of late car ferries.

Time plays for keeps here and everywhere,
though the women you loved so cryptically haven't
lost their allure: one shadow still warms the sheets
in your trysting room in Florence just the *altra* side
of the Ponte Vecchio; another lies beside a rock,
in the sun of your beloved Cinque Terre,
then slips soundlessly into the sea.

＊

We are never alone. Even while traveling we bring
a luggage-laden entourage that stretches from destination
to home and to all the homes before that. Memory sings
that Doppler song as it tests the surface tension
of water and wine, bobbing on ripples of oars
before sinking like crumbles of marble. We will never
meet, and I will never reach your stature, grand
as the statue of the *Gigante* on the beach at Monte Rosso.

But we share everything, Eugenio, we share it. Don't we?
Your Mediterranean sunflowers crazed with light,
your agaves clinging to cliffs with all the tenacity
life can muster. But if your sea is a trumpet,
Lago di Como is a reflecting pool. And I, *maestro*,
don't know whether to hold on or let go, to turn my back or
face full to the night, the moon heavy as a lemon on a tree.

STILL LIFE FROM MEMORY

It's all there—tarot laid out upon a table,
the World and the Fool, the yellow
carnation of our marriage wilting.
I have traced the faultline
to that moment in Belgium,
the bombed-out cobblestone road
when I told you I didn't know
if I could ever love anyone. From then on,
we were gypsies sleeping in the red desert,
ouds silenced, dreaming the lion.

I recall now the story you'd repeat at parties:
your Greek student shaken awake each night
by her drunken father, workingman's
revolver cocked with the reminder
that she should have been killed at birth
like the rest of the girl babies on his island.

Was that the island with the jellyfish,
Aegean waves never more than lappings?
Remember the slim balcony of our room,
how we'd sit there, *rodytis* pink as the dusk,
the turpentine taste of *retsina*, watching
wax stars drip down upon fishing boats.
And in the morning, the bells and white sheets,
coarse white goats passing, the church
glaring white at the end of the spit,
white as the wedding dress you never wore,
the name you never changed.

TRAVELERS

Creamy afternoon light in old Santa Barbara.
Drifting cigarette smoke in Aix en Provence.
The sheer humid weight of the Yucatan.
You can only be where you are.

But the couple already accepts this:
he has a nose like a wolf and a pigeon's homing compass;
she can sense a temperature shift of one degree—
there can never be enough blankets.

Picture two travelers in a hotel bed,
mattress sloping to the middle like a glacial Swiss valley
and all night long they've been boulders colliding.
Backs aching, they dress to sip green breakfast tea.

He says: "I found a dead spider in the dresser drawer,
all eight legs pointed as black knitting needles,
with the circumference of a shitake.
It looked like it had been there a long time."

She says: "They have no words for 'good luck.'
What they say is 'much rain.'"
He says: "Do you smell something burning?"
She says: "Is it cold in here?"

The waitress comes and takes their order.
He aligns knives, folds the *International Herald*.
She studies maps, rates of exchange, their tabletop world
round and flat, with edges to fall off in every direction.

LAYOVER

A traveler stranded by his wayward cock;
The ticket counters closed, bars drained and dry,
Magazine stands with grates pulled-down hard.
I wasn't going anywhere for hours.

Not even litter at the gates, just banks
Of pay phones I probably should have used.
You were right to throw me out.

Flitting with blondes at the bar in Marblehead,
The girl at the wedding dance in Vermont,
The restaurant hostess, probably more.

Were you in bed when I crossed your porch
After slipping the key in the mail slot,
Curbside taxi idling in the dark?

Beyond the wicked set of your mouth
You never let on at the meeting this morning
We ever had met or knew each other.

I had no idea you'd changed jobs, moved west.
But that project I came to pitch
Got detoured en route, flew back to Logan,
Where it sat on the runway till its wings fell off.

The Red Door

To know the red door
is not the same as stepping through.
To open the red door
and peer across the frame into a starry darkness,
the ground below indistinct, untried,
is not the same as stepping through.

༝

Bouquet in the vase on the entry table.
Chessboard of floor tile cold to bare feet.
Cups and plates quiet in kitchen cabinets,
dinner dishes unwashed in the sink.
The stifling hallway; perhaps sleeping children stir.
Bedroom windows closed to night sounds, whatever breeze.
Rumpled sheets, still slightly damp, blankets
kicked aside as if there has been a sudden decision.

༝

To dream of, to long for, the red door is not to open it.
There is no turn of a knob, click of a latch.
The red door seduces, yields easily, like lips, like legs,
hot to the touch. But with the red door,
the flirting with consequences comes before.
There is no *later*.

༝

Clothing piled on the corner chair.
Finger-smudged glass half-empty beside the mattress.
The invisible path through furniture in its accustomed places,
memorized as in a blind man's home.

The front door is not the red door.
Nor the one that leads to the yard. It doesn't slide,
no louvers, screens, or panes;
there aren't two mated halves, the upper one
thrown wide to streaming sun.

Think of the red door as a picture
projected on a beaded curtain.
Simply part the strands; black hair falling
to the small of the back, concealing
a delicate tattoo.

Of course, the red door is not always there.
It demands commitment to be seen—
there can be no hesitation. From the other side,
the red door has no color.
To find out for yourself, climb
four stairs to the threshold.

To know the red door is not the same as
stepping though.

The morning after the job loss, you drove me back
to the place we used to meet, watching the palm
fronds whisk the fog and gulls scream and shear,
the sky shrunken to a square of open sunroof.
We drank coffee, pastry flakes on our clothes,
and talked: me, murky as dock water; you, the peach
horizon and soft-focus bellies of marine clouds.
The water taxi chugged. The sportfishing boat loaded,
then put out, the aft deck milling with anglers
unemployed at least for the day, whip rods baited
and leaned over their heads like those deep-water
creatures, all mouth and teeth, that dangle appendage
lures then snap up anything attracted close enough or
simply passing. It's a fish-eat-fish world, this aquarium
we swim in, turning together in the night, a moonlit
school of two, drawing the tides up to our chins
to counter the chill that radiates through the glass.

FILTER

I wish I could explain how things
can change so quickly, a cloud engulfing
the sun, walls closing in where there are
no walls, as when I was walking my dog
in the Santa Monica Mountains and met
an elderly couple also walking their dog
to the hilltop bench with the best view.

It's difficult to remember now the warp of trail,
the buzzing chaparral, expanse of ocean visible.
I try not to focus on that one moment
when the man reached down to pat his dog
(a border collie, I think, but I'm not sure)
and his wrist extended past his sleeve.

Eucalyptus trees instantly changed their scent.
Shaggy bundles of drooping leaves
suffused with oily Australian spice suddenly
reeked of cat piss then ignited into torches,
the canopy combusted by those blue numbers
exposed to oxygen and midday heat. Sixty years
just disappeared and I heard sirens in the distance.

I don't know his story but I do.
I have no idea if Eucalyptus trees grow
on brushy Polish hillsides, but I don't think so.
I don't know how the couple found each other,
how they came to California (I didn't ask),
or how he can bear his dreams.

I only know that Eucalyptus trees and chaparral,
Sunday hikers and their dogs can fade, the filter

switched so that only one color is vivid and glows,
as if the sun had become black light,
as if a wrist had been dipped in radium
and that's all you can see when you startle awake
at the speed of transformation.

On Broken Top, Three Sisters Wilderness

I had almost forgotten the wildflowers, how they shelter
    in high mountain meadows: crimson Indian Paintbrush,
    bushy pink Monkeyflower, purple Lupine haloed
    by white airbursts of Queen Anne's Lace.

Had almost forgotten that every stream has a different voice—
    snowmelt, riffle, rocky course, waterfall—
    and how river forks slither through marshlands,
    and the semi-precious palette of glacial lakes: creamy jade;
    rusty garnet; turquoise lit from within.

Had almost forgotten the dry drum thump of boots
    treading needle mulch beneath the trunks,
    and how a Blue Noble handshake becomes a caress,
    pine pollen like cloudbanks you pass through on your way.

Had almost forgotten how life always finds a grip,
    how ferns can jimmy themselves into pumice rifts
    and Lodgepoles trace their ancestry to a seed-hold in
    a crevice, a thrusting out and then upward, and how
    growing things at altitude have stature despite clinging
    so low to the ground—dwarf architecture
    of moss, yellow broomlets of lichen, huddled heather.

Almost forgotten how the weather upslope twists
    branches not out of shape but *into* shape,
    and how the word "thistle" lisps like a breeze in the pines,
    and that sweeping aside a stone on the trail
    can veer the course of the world.

Psalm in Place of Hope

I forgive you for my aging, the coarse
White weeds among the foliage.

I forgive you for the struggles, watching others
Open their gifts then having to turn back to work.

I forgive you for all the lovely bodies I will
Never touch because you have offered me my portion.

But I reserve the right to withhold forgiveness until
Your rogue angel cells stop killing
What's already so briefly given.

I forgive you for the indecision you visit on me
And the roadblocks you send to test determination.

I forgive you for rejection and depression, for entropy
Of mind and memory, organs and the blood.

If this world is meaningless there is nothing
To forgive and forgiveness is neither yours nor mine.

I disagree with those who claim forgiveness is yours alone.
I disavow any pardon I am not part of;
Every jury will be hung.

I forgive you for the swiftness of your vengeance but
Ask why it's so often misdirected.

I forgive the swollen suffering, the unconscionable
Daily acts you allow. Where is the lesson?
It just gets worse.

Is that your plan? To foment rage and desperation
Until the fragile wings no longer bear the weight,

Until the crud and filth are caked so thickly it's easier
To close the door and wait for spontaneous combustion?
But will you then start over?

Did you simply catalyze the cycles of fire, leaf, and fruit,
Snow, flood, mud, moon, and tide? Are they random? Moot?

I look at history and cannot blame you. You have repeated
It so often it swallows itself, shits, and eats.

These questions are not to seek redress. I vent
Only to understand though I know I may never.

But if you send my mother's madness to silence me,
I swear on that disgusting pile of oil-soaked rags
In the darkest corner of my heart

I will find a way—even in decline—to incinerate
Forgiveness forever.

Dan Marino's Quick Release

There are angels if

you believe in them. Except they don't
look like angels should. They take

you in, feed and warm you, coax you on
to your next destination. Step back

for a moment from your life, see
the course, simian-like,

swinging through the trees
branch to branch—hold, float free,

branch, let go, branch, trust, branch—
the pattern if plotted on a graph

resembles a child's drawing
of ocean peaks and troughs. Or,

you can view it as the looping flight
of sparrows,

awkward burst of wingbeats followed by
gravity's glide. And repeat, kept aloft by

momentum. There is rest somewhere
(there must be), but the angels see to it

that your progress is unimpeded, fast
past those defenders far downfield,

the ball held until the last possible
second, then rifled and spiraling hard

to hit you at the crux of your cut
right between the numbers.

BORDERLINE

Mexico is bleeding people.
I am opening the sky for them.
Some smell of ochre earth.
Some are calloused as paws.
Others just refract light.
A few speak only in breezes.
I can taste the fires
in the kitchens they left behind.
Their cold matches
rattle like dried insects in my mouth.

Martín crossed near Patagonia, Arizona.
I did not open the sky for him.
Instead, I parted the river.
I walk along its banks waiting
for ocotillo to bloom; the manzanita
has such red branches...even now.
Only a *pendejo* or a *bruja* can see
beyond the chain link and flowers
with petals so large
they hide us from *la migra*.

You know what they always say:
"*El viento sobre la tierra tumba muertos.*"
Ah, yes, this land's remorseless wind
does blow away the dead.
Sunshine spills melancholy
as Martín collects rattlesnakes
and puts them in his pockets.
Puma won't sit beside him
when they stop for water—

he will stand only, tell his stories
from a distance, speak of neon cities
in some future north where it will rain
sticky money on them all.

Their haggard map points the way
to intersections with no corners.
But that's the way it is
once you pass *la linea*.
The gash is 2,000 miles long
and all the barbed wire in the world
cannot suture the wound.

Poor Dog

The dog only sees the bone
not the hand holding it.

And the donkey only the carrot,
the greyhound the mechanical hare.

The certainties remain: death,
disease, decline, and rot.

And a desire, no, longing, to be touched.
And did I mention death?

The hand holding the bone is bone within,
the stick a rigid imitation of an arm.

Now the greyhound has only three legs;
The hare ran away with a paw.

Death isn't rigid (that comes later).
It's oh-so-flexible in so many ways.

Tissue of the body is an inside joke,
organs a jumble of juices and spurts.

Trace the branching red forest:
torrents, trees, creeks, and thickets.

Is a ram in the thicket? Horn and hoof,
claw and fingernail, the last to let go.

The earth eventually gets the bone.
Death is so patient, has nothing but Time.
And now it has the dog.

ANIMAL PLANET

This is the hour of hyenas.
the hour of crows descending,
filling the trees and scaring away
the songbirds. This is the hour of
the weasels, of rampant viruses, of lap
dogs that bite your ankle as you walk away.
Now the baboons are on the loose, seizing
rocks and sticks, and the wrestling bears have
mauled their trainers. Zoo elephants crush keepers
underfoot; Seigfried and Roy have canceled tonight's
performance. It's the wrong day to wear your pet python
around your neck or to feed the piranhas by hand. Even
the dolphins are in an ugly mood—they really do have teeth
in those beaks. Lemurs and sloths are speeding up, sharpening
their long climbing nails. Prehensile tails braid tightly across
the globe. Railroad bridges, undermined by moles, collapse.
The lemmings turn back at the lip of the cliff, and beavers chew
pines to block back roads. Flocks of gulls loiter on airport runways
while winged tornadoes of flies, mosquitoes, wasps, and bees writhe
through heavy air. Listen: locusts are humming something *uber alles*.
And from the way they're waddling, the marsupials are packing heat
in their pouches. This is no walk in the woods anymore. Picnic in the park.
Hike through the bush. It's a jungle out there. Just ask the wolves, the lice,
sharks, raptors, scorpions, lizards, and voles. Is it time, Mr. Darwin? Is it time?

LAIR

Winter was my favorite.
No, not just because of the sleeping in a bundle.
Father taught us to find field mice in the snow,
to hear rustlings under the maze of dry stems,
darting feet and trembling whiskers.
I remember the white of his ruff,
snowflakes on his forehead and muzzle.
How tall he was as he reared to leap!
By the time his dewclaws broke the crust,
his jaws had snapped. We all loved
the crunch of tiny bones in our molars.

Oh, I've nearly forgotten to mention our singing,
so beautiful the stars came out just to hear it.
The woods were silken on those nights, the path
perfumed with rabbit and deer, trees with our markings.
New moon, crescent moon, half moon, full—
our tongues like ladles when we stopped
to lap at a spring.

UNLEAVENED

Take water—as much as you can pour in your hands
held hinged at the edges like a fossil shell.

Take flour. Use fingers for spoons. Pretend
they're digging claws and you're excavating a white den.

Combine water and flour until quicksand thick
and it fools you into thinking you can stand on it;
you sink in to the knees.

Close your eyes. Apply mixture liberally,
coating skin from hairline to chin.

(Important note: make appropriate holes for respiration.)

Splay yourself in the sun, preferably desert, preferably
at peak of midday. When fissures appear, remove.

Leave face behind, and begin again.

BLUR

Out east on the desert freeway,
after the rain blowing in from the coast
had been blocked by the mountains doing their work,
the sky was fearless and the sun, half arisen now,
cast shadows of slow-whirling wind turbine blades
across all eight lanes, passing over each car
like the shadow of a hunting hawk.
A man in front of a prefab church
changed letters on the sidewalk marquee.
"God is waiting..." it began but I went by too fast
to see if He was waiting for me.

Postcards to Tania From Joshua Tree

I reached the desert in record time:
windmills at dawn doing their pinwheel ballet,
then that single nowhere stoplight on route 62,
the "Roadside Bonsai" sign, the Harley diner,
and the white guardrail hidden by yellow chamisa
on the entrance road to the park.

⁓

A lizard rustles through the brush
dragging a tail so long I thought at first it was
a snake going backwards. The sky here
bursts with blue. And at the campground picnic table
a scrub jay was blue with waiting.

⁓

The desert dictates, takes you over.
It breathes for you like a respirator;
my chest begins to rise and fall
at geologic pace.

⁓

I realize how exhausted I am.
I need to sleep, even if standing up,
nuisance flies shooed with an involuntary
quiver of dorsal muscle or twitch of an erect ear.
Do the insects ever stop, ever just light someplace?
Do things ever stay put, flat as varnish stain on granite,
not metamorphic rock but rock at rest, in stasis?
The white floral pincushions nod that, yes, this is possible.
And moments later they are proven right by a jackrabbit

who emerges from a nearby bush paying me no attention
because no part of me, including my mind, is in motion.

༐

My body is just a scuted shell with ribs attached,
so small now and dense
even a dewdrop of thought can't wedge into
the fissures to freeze and cause
fragmentation.

༐

Focus narrows to Joshua seed size,
stopped down to desert aperture, irises constricted
by purity of light. I am thronged by tiny wildflowers,
a wet winter's generosity scattered from sea clouds
blown inland.

༐

Reminders are everywhere of my own reduction:
gritty yellow grains of Mormon tea pollen,
compact tufts of mistletoe in the acacias.
Yet I am not diminished, but, rather, concentrated—
more than before with so much less volume
despite the vast poultice that envelops me,
tries to draw me out of my pores
like the desert perspiration you never see.

Perception. Filters. Screens.
The way a smoke tree looks.
The way I now see the name,
letters like smoke venting from my mouth:
smoke treeeeeee.
The image it makes in my mind
that I so easily inhabit.

I feel fused to the pink quartz of this boulder, its mass
attracting, pulling me in. Would I enter
if a passage widened to a cavern,
would I leave this plane knowing I could never go back?
The windshield of my car glints in the sun
an easy walk away.

THREE FATES

I. Weaver

A white egret flies under a white bridge,
gray legs stretched out behind and for a moment
pauses the morning fog
and the creep of tide up the banks,
the cruciform reflection of the egret,
the white arch of the footbridge
(which is water and which is sky
and which is warped by barely perceptible
ripples of something feeding below?),
the egret's flight defining architecture of light
and bridge, the passage of water to ocean and back,
the daylight moon setting behind leaf-barren trees,
the sun rising above a house that exudes
a piano concerto through curtains open to the canal
where sleeping sea ducks float, heads tucked,
necks so much stockier than the egret's,
which is like thick white cord threaded to
the yellow beak, sewing the air to the water,
the water to the bridge, the bridge to the bank,
through the loops of music, the fabric of fog,
the braided sticks and down of pouchy swallow nests
hung beneath the concrete arch
where now the white wings of the egret emerge,
drawing all above and all below into
something tight and seamless.

II. *Allotter*

This is what we are given:

years like floating leaf haiku,
candle boats on the current,

the same current that erodes the banks
and makes them crumble in muddy chunks,

scooping larger and larger until
the bow of the river takes a sweeping turn

and we miss the years passing out of reach,
distracted by the jigging of red crawfish.

A full heart, then an empty home.
A full belly, then nothing left to devour.

The body betrays the mind.
The mind betrays the heart.

And memory betrays them all,
the river a white lie

sent to ease the transition.

III. Not Turning Back

Luminescent squid risen
to just beneath the surface are memories.
The waves are seasons,
one after the other, reaching farther and farther
up the beach. The squid, moon, and waves
collude with the undertow of the past,
pulling you steadily out to depth.

And you've always wanted to take this time,
to ponder how it is you came to be treading:
the choices and branchings;
the charities of coincidence;
bundles put down or picked up,
how far you were willing to carry them.

Your sister, your sister, your sister,
your mother trying to outshout the sea.
Your wives, your father
disapproving, approving, silent from the grave.

Decisions made in shallows,
the courses changed, stayed, corrected,
sometimes rowing, sometimes
just giving in to the drift. The wind a lull,
the wind a friend pushing from behind,
and then even the wind against you.

The water is woven with squid,
faint blue glimmers under the swells
that stretch to the horizon,
which is the edge of a box that holds

the whole arc of bay, all the teeming sea,
and in its lid are tiny pinpricks where light
from somewhere else leaks through.

PICKING FRUIT IN THE DARK

Oranges, pink grapefruit, blueberry pearls
and strawberries big as plums . . .

The boat has floated in again,
run aground far up the shore,
its anchor line frayed and unsecured,
its passenger patiently waiting.

A man sporting a straw boater strolls by,
one good aqueous eye,
in his teeth a pipe; lost thoughts
trail him like puffs of smoke.

He resembles my grandfather, mother's side—
telltale moustache, heavy wingtip shoes,
collar and wool suit
despite the rising heat.

I didn't even know he could row.
Yet he unships the oars and, barely breaking
a sweat, skims the sand, disappears
into the convolutions of a shell.

. . .bing cherries and cling peaches,
cantaloupe perfume . . .

The house overlooking the beach
seems empty, but generations
have summered there, or now recline
in hospice chaises, too weak to read.

Women wear embroidered dresses,
white on white on white,
fresh and starched from drying on a line.
They sit composed, sewing without thread.

I don't recognize any of them—
mother, sister, daughter, or wife.
Perhaps I'll encounter them on the lawn
or at tea on Sunday afternoon.

Poetry and a violin. Or is it cicada sawing?
No young men at all.
There must be war on the horizon,
night harvest in another foreign land.

*. . . yellow Philippine mangoes, Mexican red papaya,
pear apples from Japan . . .*

To hold white petals before they fall,
delay the ripening, the fruiting season.
If only I'd been earlier
to make sense of such profusion.

Faux Sestina Flanked by Fragments From Sappho

Memories
terribly leaked away . . .

not a flood but a steady faucet drip,
too quiet a shadow to disturb any sleep,
the hairline in the levee spidering
and a terrible pressure building behind,
each drop joining a slow spherical sequence,
a liquid lens reflecting the past,

hanging, dangling, suspended
until a collusion of gravity, mass, and time
makes it loosen and let go,
slow passage through the air,
the terrible suspense
when we are least ourselves to view its plummet

from creation to obliteration,
which is, after all,
the fate of memories,
which are, after all,
the shadows of our living;
memories form, accumulate, pool, and leak,

a sequence without deviation,
the little finger pricked by a thorn
that won't stop bleeding...
and aren't memories like blood
recirculating, contained, sealed
in a shadowy hydraulic system

until something silent as
a spider causes it to leak
and the sequence of our history
ruptures like an aneurism in the brain,

the glittery particles once held in suspension
drifting to the silted bottom—

leaves, gold flecks, feathers lost
for someone else to happen upon, perhaps to acquire;
our living, I say, diminishes
but does not completely perish
and even when there is nothing more to leak
and we slow the sequence of struggle,

the venom beginning to work
suspended in the terrible spider web of shadow,
even if we cannot ourselves...

someone will remember us,
I say,
even in another time.

THE HALF-LIFE OF MEMORY

It's as toxic as any nuclear mountain,
though it's a mountain that comes to you.
It's not out there beside some wasted stretch
of Nevada 50 or among the radioactive rabbits
on the high plains of eastern Washington
where tumbleweeds choke the fences
and little rodent deaths foul the wells.

You are the soldier it was tested on,
the shadow vaporized onto the wall.
Take off your goggles, your safe
white suit, ignore the Geiger's jittering.
To look back is to risk becoming salt
like the lining of subconscious dumps
half a mile beneath southern New Mexico.

Its waning anticipates yours.
It decays before your bags are even packed,
was last seen traveling toward the vanishing point
of a half-lived life. A mirror with degraded silver,
you see through it but not back.
It is spent fuel, seems benign and clean,
sweet-talks you into thinking exposure won't burn.

But even showers of alkaline regret
can't prevent contamination.
You don't have enough years to wait it out,
enough concrete to contain it.

Photographic Memory

The problem is not that people remember through photographs,
but that they remember only the photographs.

—Susan Sontag

I.

When the fire
was almost to our house,
the flames just a ridge
and a whim of the wind away,

after the sheriff's car
had rolled past blaring
over the too-loud loudspeaker
that we should prepare to flee,

it was then we had to make
our choices,
what we couldn't live without,
what was irreplaceable.

And after the wind had shifted
and our neighborhood was spared,
and we were left wringing out
the dinge of smoke

and the images of blackened
trees along the fire line
like dead sentries
at their posts, and the houses

had been hung with sheets
painted to thank the firefighters,
it was then we felt
secure enough

to unpack the car, still freighted
and pointing downhill.
And, later, in the parking lots
and grocery stores,

in the telephone conversations
repeated with each neighbor,
each worried inquiring
relative and friend, the question

was the same, fueled
by vicarious urgency,
a searing curiousity:
What did you take?

And always, among the pets and art,
legal papers and financial records,
cash, heirlooms, and jewelry,
the answer was: *the photographs.*

II.

After the second fireball had singed us all
and the world had turned into a negative,
after the images had been replayed, replayed,
and replayed until we could replay them
at unwilling will, and after the ash had elbowed
through the streets and the flurries of business
paper had drifted and the face of the devil
had been traced in the smoke and the leaping bodies
had embraced gravity one final time
and were not orderly in their fall like bowler-hatted
Magritte men and were not surreal but all too real,
and the gray tentacles had engulfed the buildings
and pulled until they collapsed, and after
the smoldering and the compressed eternity
of digging, dismantling, and disposal,
when hope had been sifted and sorted,
and there were not hands to go with fingers
wearing rings set with stones born and returned
to the heat and pressure, after the tattered flags
and the incessant nights of seeing and coughing,
vigils beside posters grieving on chain link fences,
the photographs from desks and wallets and walls
were found and restored, were survivors
in place of survivors.

III.

In the photograph on my desk, my daughter at nine years old
stands beside my dog, a crescent of empty beach in the background.
Both are looking out to sea, the dog's belly fur dripping
from a foray into the surf, tongue lapping up the briney water
that I never understood how he could drink. The sand they stand on
is wet from a just-receded wave and reflects the clouds the way
the salt flats west of Salt Lake City do and you feel
you are walking on the sky turned upside down
or on a glass negative, everything reversed except time.

IV.

The verb is to *take* a picture,
as if to own it, just as a camera

is feared to steal a shard of soul.
We cannot possess the past,

even in snapshot fragments.
We cannot possess anything, although

we can be possessed with possessing,
or, rather, attempting to possess.

Videos, prints, slides, rounds
of home movies on outmoded film

like a pantry full of cookie tins
from Christmases past, or family

albums stacked and neglected
as leather-bound ledgers on

rural assessor's shelves;
an infinitesimal aperture, the present

hoarded against summer's fade.
Already the fireflies are dead in the jar.

V.

The world gone virtual.
The world gone digital.
The whole disposable world
seen through a viewfinder,
a transparency structured on sparks,
stop-action wingbeats
with one singled out.
And this is what I'll remember.
And this...

Come back to me, my minutes.
Come back to me, my sweet aging,
the sprocketed path I have traveled.
The photographs are the proof,
aren't they, kept safe from the fire,
the irrefutable truth of *I was* and *I am*.
The rest is just music in winter air—
not even there. It's not even there.

In Memory of Her Memory

The caterpillar on the leaf
Repeats to thee thy mother's grief.
                            —William Blake

IN MEMORY OF HER MEMORY

I.

Grieve now. The woman you knew as your mother is gone,
mind shutting down lobe by lobe,
the summer house closed for good.

She loved to talk. She loved Lake Michigan's beach,
and, finally, the dry and bouldery San Diego hillsides thick
with rabbits and birds, the lavish bushes outside her rooms.
She loved meetings, agendas, committees.
But I never interfere, she insisted.

She pushed me to learn tennis with a gift
of a Green Stamp racquet, took lessons with me
on cracked public courts, embarrassing me,
the fat boy, to play hard, to be better.

A beautiful day was her glory, crowing
spectacular weather to us as if
our senses were failing.

She sits with eyes closed, slumped
to the bad-shoulder side of her locked wheelchair
watching storms gather—or abate—on the prairies
of her inner eyelids; me, folded and uncomfortable
on the floral couch facing her, my reflection
on the hard marble floor. I remind her I'm there,
that she can open her eyes and talk to me.
About what?, she asks.

II.

Should we talk about the small fruit you always favored?
Not small like kumquats or round key limes, but small
as in *concentrate*, as if the fruit sugar has been compressed
into essence to intensely pleasure the tongue. Or, perhaps,
small as in *almost ripe*, the sweetness of youth on the verge
of encountering bittersweet, what is waiting under the tree,
the fallen fruit more than allegory, more than proof of gravity.
Or, perhaps, it's the small of *reduction*, as of expectations—
art school unaffordable, never going to Europe, never owning
that Cadillac, income dwindled from moderate to just enough
to cover, seeing your children grown, moved away, not stricken.

III.

You moved away ever so slowly, a slight
loosening of the first ring joint, then the little
finger.

My father, beloved husband in granite, pulls
you down beside him as if into an unmade
bed.

Ten years you've fasted without him, loosening
like skin over brittle bone, like faces threaded to
names.

What you were holding you don't want anymore:
clothes grown too big, purses, beads, shelves of
shoes.

I fixed it, your favorite, twice. A new white band,
later, a battery. But it stopped almost willfully, that
watch.

How does a leaf know when to let go? *A horse
going back to the stable*, you used to say. *I'm
home.*

IV.

The horse that is my mother's memory
has run away. It hasn't gone far;
we can see it standing on the hill beside
our property, a silhouette at twilight.
I don't know who feeds or curries it now,
or if it has gone completely feral.
Sometimes the horse will come close, stand
just out of rope's reach. She calls to it,
then whispers of their past together.
The horse nickers and snorts softly
when she mentions Philadelphia or Chicago.
Its long neck extends and the horse shakes
its head when she talks about my father,
how she misses him, how people still
stop her on the street or in the grocery store
to tell her they miss him, too.
The horse doesn't seem to mind
that she repeats herself so often. No one
recalls when the horse got out
or who left the stable door open,
but perhaps the horse will return on its own
and we'll find it early one morning in its stall
munching hay and burnished oats.
We'll stroke the velvet blaze on its forehead,
reach into our back pockets
for those special carrots it loves.
And, if we're lucky, the horse
will linger for a while, maybe
lead us to the place where it last saw
my mother's missing hearing,
which also slipped away silently
while we were all asleep.

V.

You stumble sleepless into afternoon, ask (no, *plead*) for release.
Daydreams become hallucinations and sweet rest barrels away
like a train coming out of the fireplace at exactly 12:43
only to pull into an empty station. Vacant windows
fill with shadows, which are hints the sun keeps dropping.

You realize you're mired in time, each day sentenced
to repeat the lunar cycle, new moon dark to dark side of full,
consumed with visions of gray heads lolling in hallways
obscured by curtains and fog, singing circadian roundabouts,
singing circadian roundabouts, until all fall down.

You pace the platform, helpless to stanch what is happening
on the other side of the continent. Beneath a sign that promises
"Track 17 to Babylon" you wait for the light of the train.
Her hospital seems so much like the tunnel, tracks disappearing
around an exhausted curve. You wonder how long before it comes.

VI.

I wonder how long you will lay
on that Emergency Room gurney, eyes closed,
broken at the hip and in so many other ways.
I only know that you, disoriented traveler rushed
by ambulance in what may as well have been
a foreign land, are no longer with me.

Your face takes on tranquility
I've seen just once before—a white Rodin marble
called "Last Vision"—and then your hands become
a girl's again, supple and gently stroking
something that has come to lay upon your breast.

Could my father be there with you, his ear
to your shallow respiration that I, too, can monitor,
but with senses bound to this technical dimension,
a calibrated screen of peaks and valleys,
andante processional of quiet beeps?

Or is it a cat upon your sternum,
sleek and purring, suddenly
material and pressing down
with a warmth and weight I cannot fathom
and must wait my turn to feel?

Your hands still, their backs already
purpling from intravenous needles, arms
and tubes limp again along the confines
of the mattress edge.

I do not hear the leaving
of whatever was on your chest,
could not see it pad away,

tight to the wall of the corridor
and skittish among the paramedics rushing in
with more downed bodies, more hushed wheels.

And now there's no way to ask
if it had your green eyes.

VII.

Our eyes, it's said, are the same eyes we have as children.
They simply fail, they don't change or age.
unlike the marred veneer, abraded by a thousand rivers,
ten thousand rapids roiling.

I dream a murky voice explaining
that a date must be set for placement
of my father's stone, we must choose a location
(though the exact word, I recall, was *community*).
Angry and confused, I blurt:
He already has a gravestone. He's 10 years buried.
Then I become concave with doubt. Is this yet another
Jewish ritual, more words to pronounce phonetically
with no meaning but circumstance, but context,
more mirrors to cover in mourning,
as if to see me is not to see you?

VIII.

I see you there, not in *the* home, but in *our* home,
bundled in a white afghan on a white couch—alert, lucid, heart
rate returned and hip mended, asking questions again
that actually matter, recognizing all in the room
and reweaving the mesh.

I wait for the inevitable, for you to turn the wheel
of the conversation, for the bottle somehow to spin to you
and pour out all the old stories running like consecutive chapters
of Saturday serials you watched with Polly, Golda, and Bea,
each dissolving into each, endings to be continued—how you sat
outcast in the pews while they made their confessions,
how the French teacher thought you could *parlez*
because your name was spelled Bien (but pronounced "bean"
by your English family), how you designed jewelry without
taking a class, drafted M-4 tanks among the men left at home,
how you met my father at a wedding and thought him
the handsomest man in the world, how you took him
to wedding after wedding until he got the idea...

Even in dreams I never thought I'd be glad to see
those rusty cars coupled again,
the steaming locomotive we learned to derail
before it gained momentum.

But awake again, relief drains. I hear the Sunday papers delivered,
whumping the pavement as if dropped from great height.

I check the bedside clock, the alarm that hasn't buzzed,
and the phone that hasn't yet rung to convey the dreaded words,
that too-early call I know is coming, that rides my shoulders
like Chagall's small rabbi, his legs clenched tight 'round my neck,
his beard tangled in my hair.

IX.

So distracted, so tangled with humdrum—
the morning brushing of teeth, the
inconsequential—I remember now
how the ringing phone annoyed me.

Your mother's heart failed,
the doctor said,
completely.

Mother, you finally ran fast enough
to catch your fleeing memory. The body
you leave behind is of no use anymore,
like the view of the two perfect palm trees
when I'd look up from my book in your room,
or the telephone pole clothed in greenery where
crows perched, dignified and silent for once.
Flocks of pigeons flew past your window.
Nurses with exotic names changed shifts,
Indonesian, Philippino, a Russian with you
when you tasted your last Earth air
at 7 A.M., the hour you gave me
life.

You chose a good day to die,
windy as the old days in Chicago and clear,
the beach sand near my house drifted into miniature dunes,
one after the other west to the waves.
The mountains also arrived in sets, one after another
as I summitted Sepulveda Pass,
the hospital looming unmistakable in the valley below
black and dense as a cosmic hole
I had to enter to deal with the details of
death,

I signed papers, made phone calls and arrangements,
spoke silent words to the ceiling before they took you away,
then walked back out through the automatic doors, into
what might as well have been the other side of the
universe.

Epilogue

On the other side of your grave there were words
on the chairs, too many words in Hebrew transliteration
mounded too high beside the white canopy on the hill
too steep for a funeral. The shovel was too shiny
and your coffin too small and too heavy,
and the hole in the ground did not seem as deep
as the O of your mouth between sunken cheeks.
There were too many people whose names
we had to remember, too few still alive,
and so many too infirm to attend.
There was too much supplication and rending
of black ribbon, too many white roses
and pink-tinged roses and purple irises laid on the lid.
There were too many birds bunching in flocks and
too few clouds. It was too hot for dark suits
and there was no shade. The limousine
was too long and its windows too tinted to see,
the procession too short leaving the cemetery,
and our Kaddish too raw to tell blessing from loss,
descent and decline from arising.

Now, grieve now. Now, grieve now.
The woman you knew as your mother is gone.

NOTES

"RAIN IN L.A.": MOVIES, MUSIC, AND INSPIRATIONS

Thursday morning: "Red Wind," a short story by Raymond Chandler; *The Maltese Falcon*; "So What" by Miles Davis on the album *Kind of Blue*; *The Wizard of Oz*.

Thursday evening: *Cool Hand Luke*; *Othello* by William Shakespeare; *Them*.

Middle of the night: *The Big Sleep* by Raymond Chandler; *Body Heat*.

Friday dawn: "The eagles flies on Friday" comes from "Stormy Monday Blues," sung by Buddy Guy on the album *My Time After Awhile*; "The Blues Is My Business" is on Larry McCray's album *Believe It!*; "I'm so broke right now I can't even spend the night" comes from "Too Broke to Spend the Night" sung by Buddy Guy on the album *Damn Right I Have the Blues*; I sure wish I could find out the name of the song with the lyrics "I ordered coffee, but the blues poured me misery," which I heard on Long Beach radio station KJZZ one day while sitting in a Costco parking lot; "I feel like I'm drowning on dry land" comes from "Drowning on Dry Land" by Roy Buchanan on the album *The Alligator Records 20th Anniversary Collection*; "Somebody got to suffer, somebody sure got to feel some pain" comes from "Love, Life and Money" by Johnny Winter on the album *The Alligator Records 25th Anniversary Collection*; "…you may wash your life away" comes from "Laundromat Blues" sung by Carey Bell on the album *Living Chicago Blues, Vol. 1*.

Friday late afternoon: *Armageddon;* "Take It Easy," versions by Jackson Browne and The Eagles; "Wicked Rain" is on the album *Kiko* by Los Lobos; "Two Trains Running," many versions, including the Butterfield Blues Band on the album *East-West*, James Cotton on his album *Deep in the Blues*, and The Blues Project on their *Anthology* release.

Saturday morning: *Key Largo*; "I Love L.A.," composed and sung by Randy Newman.

Saturday sunset: "Casida of the Branches" by Federico García Lorca, translated by Stephen Spender and J. L. Gili; "Rain," a short story by Somerset Maugham; "Cry Me a River" sung by Julie London on the Rhino album *Sirens of Song*; *The Treasure of Sierra Madre*; *Monty Python and the Holy Grail*, with apologies to René Descartes.

Saturday night: *Who'll Stop the Rain* is a film based on Robert Stone's novel, *Dog Soldiers*, and a song by Credence Clearwater Revival on their album *Chronicle*; *The Killers*.

Sunday: "Lament for Ignacio Sánchez Mejías" by Federico García Lorca, translated by Stephen Spender and J. L. Gili; "Born in Chicago" is on the album *The Paul Butterfield Blues Band*; "Serves Me Right to Suffer" by Jimmy Johnson is on the album *The Alligator Records 20th Anniversary Collection*; *Casablanca*; *Out of the Past*; *Night and the City*; *Chinatown*.

Sunday noon: *Unforgiven*; *Fear Strikes Out*; "Put the Blame on Mame" from *Gilda*, sung by Rita Hayworth in the movie, but the voice is Anita Ellis'; "Pico and Sepulveda," originally recorded in 1947 by Felix Figueroa and his Orchestra, is now only available on the album *Banda en Fuego* by Lee Press-on and the Nails; *I Want to Live!*; *Sunset Boulevard*.

PICKING FRUIT IN THE DARK

The epigraph in "Memory and Rain" is from James Sallis' novel *Moth*.

"The Red Door" was inspired by a painting by Prescott, AZ, artist Dave Newman.

"On Broken Top, Three Sisters Wilderness" is for James Farrell.

"Dan Marino's Quick Release" is inspired by Dan Marino, a Pro Football Hall of Fame quarterback, who played for the Miami Dolphins from 1983-1999. He was known for his quick release—i.e. his speed in setting up after the snap of the ball, finding his receiver, and throwing a pass.

The quote in Spanish in "Borderline" comes from Jaime Sabines' lyrics to the song "Mi Corazón Me Recuerda" on the album *Border/La Linea* by Lila Downs.

The fragments quoted in "Faux Sestina Flanked by Fragments From Sappho" are from *If Not, Winter,* Sappho's poetry translated by Anne Carson.

The epigraph in "Photographic Memory" is from Susan Sontag's *Regarding the Pain of Others.*

About the Author

Jim Natal is the author of two previous poetry collections, *Talking Back to the Rocks* and *In the Bee Trees*, which was a finalist for the Pen Center USA and Publisher's Marketing Association Ben Franklin Awards. His poetry was nominated for a 2007 Pushcart Prize and has appeared in many journals and anthologies. A former executive of the National Football League's Creative Services Group, he also curated poetry series in Los Angeles for 10 years. In 2004, he co-founded Conflux Press with his wife, book artist Tania Baban. He currently teaches creative writing at Yavapai College in Prescott, AZ, where he also servers as the director of the Hassayampa Institute's The Literary Southwest series.